spot

ARCTIC ANIMALS

SEA OTTERS

by Anastasia Suen

AMICUS | AMICUS INK

fur

whiskers

Look for these words and pictures as you read.

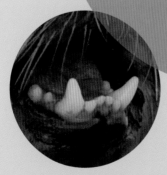

teeth

foot

What is on that ice?

It's a sea otter.

Sea otters live in the water.
They float in groups.
The groups are called rafts.

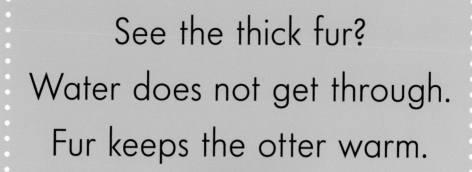

See the thick fur?
Water does not get through.
Fur keeps the otter warm.

fur

whiskers

See the whiskers?

They feel for food underwater.

They find clams.

teeth

See the teeth?
They are sharp.
They open shells.
Crack!

See the foot? It is flat.
The toes are webbed.
This helps the otter swim.

foot

A new pup is born.
It is fluffy. It rides on mom.

See the thick fur?
Water does not get through.
Fur keeps the otter warm.
fur

fur

whiskers
See the whiskers?
They feel for food underwater.
They find clams.

whiskers

Did you find?

teeth

teeth
See the teeth?
They are sharp.
They open shells.
Crack!

foot

See the foot? It is flat.
The toes are webbed.
This helps the otter swim.
foot

Spot is published by Amicus and Amicus Ink
P.O. Box 1329, Mankato, MN 56002
www.amicuspublishing.us

Library of Congress Cataloging-in-Publication Data
Names: Suen, Anastasia, author.
Title: Sea otters / by Anastasia Suen.
Description: Mankato, Minnesota : Amicus/Amicus Ink,
   [2020] | Series: Spot arctic animals | Audience: K to
   Grade 3.
Identifiers: LCCN 2018048669 (print) | LCCN 2018049063
   (ebook) | ISBN 9781681518398 (pdf) | ISBN
   9781681517995 (library binding) | ISBN 9781681525273
   (paperback)
Subjects: LCSH: Sea otter—Juvenile literature. | Animals—
   Arctic regions—Juvenile literature.
Classification: LCC QL737.C25 (ebook) | LCC QL737.C25
   S7758 2020 (print) | DDC 599.769/5—dc23
LC record available at https://lccn.loc.gov/2018048669

Printed in China

HC 10 9 8 7 6 5 4 3 2 1
PB 10 9 8 7 6 5 4 3 2 1

Alissa Thielges, editor
Deb Miner, series designer
Ciara Beitlich, book designer
Holly Young and Shane Freed,
   photo researchers

Photos by Superstock/Suzi Eszterhas
cover, 16; Shutterstock/allixout
1; Shutterstock/Jim Schwabel 3;
Newscom/Thomas Kline 4–5;
ScienceSource/Tom & Pat Leeson
6–7; Alamy/Kevin G. Smith/Alaska
Stock 8–9; Newscom/Rebecca
Jackrel/DanitaDelimont.com 10–11;
Shutterstock/Menno Schaefer 12–13;
Shutterstock/Manuel Balesteri 14–15

SEA OTTERS